THE SHY ARTIST'S GUIDE TO

The 10 Biggest
(and Totally Avoidable)

Mistakes
that Keep
You From
Being a
Successful
Artist

Loretta Alvarado

How Original! Publishing - Mission Viejo, California, U.S.A.

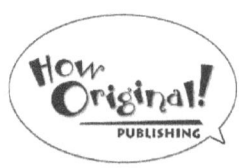

How Original! Publishing
Mission Viejo, CA 92691
949-415-4749
info@howoriginal.net

ISBN: 1507576102
ISBN-13: 978-1507576106

Table of Contents

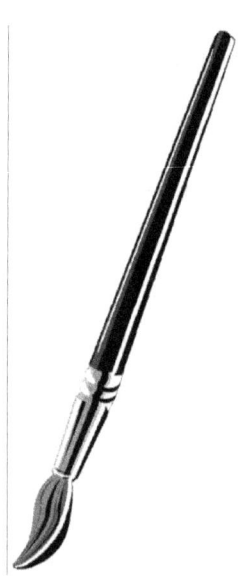

The Shy Artist's Guide to

The 10 Biggest (and Totally Avoidable) Mistakes That Keep You From Being a Successful Artist

Introduction

As artists, we all make mistakes, sometimes lots of them. It is not that we are any less or more intelligent than non-artists. It is that we tend to work in our own compartmentalized world...a studio, a quiet room, a scenic location...somewhere we can be isolated with our art. Not having the constant 9 to 5 interaction with our peers means not having that instant feedback when we do make a mistake. This leads to those mistakes continuing unabated. And, they can hamper your success as an artist.

There are many barriers that an artist has to overcome in order to be successful. Not only do you have to create the product, you also have to package it, market it, sell it, deliver it, and follow up. Any of these steps can result in a mistake.

But there are certain things that all artists do regardless of whether they are selling their work through shows, selling through a gallery, selling online, exhibiting, or even just giving art away as gifts. These are mistakes that are common to artists in general. You may not have made all of these mistakes during your art career, but I'm sure you've made at least one.

See if your recognize yourself in any of the following. If you do, then it may be wise for you to do something about it. In these pages, I have identified ten (plus one bonus!) of the biggest mistakes that artists make. I have described them and given examples so you can see if any of them fit you. And I have provided action steps for you to do to correct these mistakes.

I hope that this information will help to improve not only your art, but also your art career. And, to help you out even more visit: www.TheShyArtist.com/mistakes for your FREE bonus which I will tell you about in a later chapter.

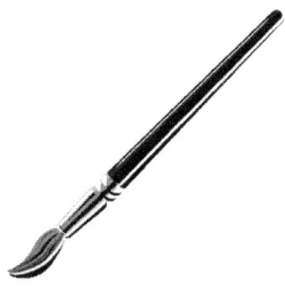

Mistake #1: Not having a voice

Many years ago when I first started out doing art shows, I decided that in order to keep my work fresh, new and interesting from year to year, I would change my theme. So, every year I would pick some theme that I wanted to work with and I created all of my art around that theme. One year it was cats. The next it was dragons. Another year it was music. And then I went to ocean. I found that it was much easier to work within the confines of a theme.

However, here is the problem: Every year I would get customers coming up to me and asking if it was my first year at that show.

They didn't recognize my work! They didn't connect my new theme and my work with the previous year's theme. They thought I was a new artist.

Needless to say, I no longer change my theme every year. Now I have one main theme that I always show. It happens to be music. I will add some other things in just to experiment and see if they get any attention. But overall, what I have become known for is my music art.

So, what does it mean to have a voice?

Having a voice is showing the world who you are. It is that instantly recognizable style, quality, or whatever it is that says this is a Picasso or this is a Rembrandt.

You know you have attained that quality when you first hear from someone who sees your work and says, "I saw your work at such-and-such a show."

It feels really good to have your work recognized. But even more important, now that your work is recognized, people will remember it. Once they remember it, you have just increased the chances of making a sale.

So how do you find your voice?

Practice.

I know it seems like a simplistic answer, but it is true. The more work you create, the more you begin to find what excites you. That excitement helps you identify your passion. And the more your work tends toward your passion, the sooner you will find your voice.

It's about creating a consistent and cohesive body of work. It's about having a body of work that flows from one piece to the next without jarring the eye. It's about having a body of work in the same style, technique, medium, or theme.

This does not mean that you can't do work in other styles, techniques, media, or themes. Even Picasso had his Blue Period and his Cubism Period. It just means that whenever you show your work in public, put out the work that is similar. Unless of course, you are doing a complete retrospective of your entire body of work, in which case, you will probably want to group similar works together.

Action Step
Look at your entire body of work. See if you can find a consistent theme or style that is common to much of it or all of it. Now, determine what it is about the theme or style that makes you keep creating art. This is your passion. Keep creating art using this passion and you will find your voice.
Note: if you can't really find any theme or style, then just find SOMETHING in your work that makes you smile, or feel some sort of strong emotion. That will do just as well for a starting point.

Mistake #2: Underselling

Many years ago, I juried into a major arts festival with a large art quilt. I was talking to one of the people in charge. She asked how much I was going to sell this piece for. I wasn't sure. I scratched my head a minute and thought, well, I've got about $75 worth of materials in this piece, so $150. That was the number I spit out. And she said, "Oh, that's a good price."

So that was the price tag I put on it. Opening Night, I had two people who wanted it. And I sold it for $150. I made another one and I sold the second one for $150 because they had already seen it at that price. I have since made several versions of this design and I now sell it at $1500.

There is a lot of time involved in this piece. There's design work because it's an original design. There are materials costs, the cost of the electricity, the cost of me driving to go buy the fabric, etc. There are lots of costs that go into making something. And it's not just the materials.

Don't forget that you have spent a lot of time practicing and honing your skills. It may have taken you 10 hours to complete a piece, but there was a lot of time that went into learning the skills and techniques necessary to complete it.

Let me relate an example of extreme underselling. I was at a small weekend show. The lady in the booth next to me made jewelry. Every time someone would walk into her booth she would proudly explain that her prices were so low because she only charged for her materials.

Interesting business model. And, a good way to go out of business fast. Think about this for a moment. What if she got all of her materials for free? If we extrapolate to a ridiculous extent, then according to her stated "business model" she would be giving away all of her work for nothing! That certainly doesn't make any sense, does it?

Be sure to factor all of your costs into the price of your work. Include not just the cost of the materials, but also the costs to produce the work, and the costs of doing the shows, and the costs of marketing, and all of the other costs that go into running your art business.

Action Step
Do some research. Visit an art show or look online and find several different artists whose work is similar to yours. How much are their pieces selling for? If your prices are substantially different, then maybe you need to rethink your pricing structure. Also, consider having pieces in a variety of price points. Not everyone can afford the $5,000 original, but they may be able to afford the $100 reproduction.

Mistake #3: Not having (or having and not using) a mailing list

Do you keep a guest book in your booth during shows? Do you collect email addresses from your website? Do you send out notices of your upcoming shows? If not, why not?

Having a mailing list is the single best way to sell your work. Why? Because you are bringing yourself to the attention of potential customers every time you send them something. And, the more they see you, the more they remember you, and the more likely they are to buy from you sometime in the future.

Out in the world today there is such a glut of promotional information and advertising bombarding people. You have to do something to cut through all of that clutter and differentiate your message from the noise and sound-bites. Sending out a monthly newsletter is a great way to do this. Fill it with useful and timely information. For example, at the beginning of your art show season, send out a newsletter with an article that talks about "Three tips to get the most out of an art show." Or how about "Easy and inexpensive ways to frame that piece of art you just purchased."

If you are an outdoor photographer an article like "How to have the best experience at ..." is a great way to talk about some place that you just went to. For a jeweler, an article like "What's the best outfit to wear with that new necklace?" will give you an opportunity to give more details about a new piece you just created.

I'm sure you can come up with lots of ideas like this. Even if you don't write an article for every newsletter that you send out, you can at least send out your upcoming art show schedule.

The point is that you need to get your name in front of people as much as possible without being intrusive. Offer your potential patrons a glimpse into your creative world, to make them feel they're part of a select group that really understands your art.

If you already are collecting names and keeping a mailing list, good for you! My question to you is: are you keeping it current? This is one mistake I myself keep making, even after many years as a professional artist.

I collect all those names, show after show...and then I don't put them into my list until I absolutely need them. By the time I start typing them into my mailing list spreadsheet, I have completely forgotten why I got the person's name in the first place.

I send out annual opening-night invitations to the big art show I do every year, and it is extremely embarrassing to have someone come up to you and say, "Oh, that piece I saw at your earlier show is so beautiful that I just have to buy it for the space by my fireplace...I don't see it here tonight...you remember the piece, don't you?" and you have no idea what they are talking about. Was it the enormous $10,000 seascape? Or was it the colorful $10.00 greeting card? Keeping your mailing list up-to-date can be a great way to augment your memory.

The trick with a mailing list is to input the information as soon as possible so that you can add your own notes and recollections about the person. The more information you have about that person, the more personal you can be when you send them something. For example, if they were looking

13

at that special specific piece, you can send them an email with a picture of it and let them know you now have it available as a reproduction.

Action Step
Buy a guest book or create one. Put it out at every show or exhibit. Whether you use old fashioned index cards or a fancy computer program, store the information. Send out periodic mailings to the people on your list.

Bonus – Newsletter Topic Ideas

Visit: **www.theshyartist.com/mistakes**

and download your free list of newsletter topic ideas. These ideas can also be used for blog posts or for posting to social media.

Mistake #4: Showing everything you have ever created

Have you ever seen a booth that was so cluttered with work that you didn't know where to look? I used to have one of those booths. I thought that I had to put everything in there that I have ever made. Every style, every size, every color, just everything. What happened was there was so much stuff that no one knew what my art was about. My voice (see Mistake #1) was drowned out.

Here's another question: Ever go to a store looking to buy something and you were presented with so many different choices that you were overwhelmed and couldn't pick which item to get? So you walked out without buying anything.

It's the same thing with your booth. If you present people with too many choices, they won't be able to decide. I know that many beginning artists (and even some seasoned professionals!) fall into this trap. I certainly have. The inclination is to want to have all your available work visible so that whatever catches the eye of a potential buyer will be right there.

In many art show venues, galleries and other exhibit spaces, the area of space that you have to display your work is limited. You have to carefully choose what goes on your walls. If you don't then it is hard to capture the attention of your potential customers because they won't know where to look.

Having a cluttered booth is confusing. Instead, give people an aesthetically pleasing display to rest their eyes upon.

The best way to present your work is to think of yourself as a curator at a museum. You want to present your viewing public with a cohesive body of work that all fits together. Whether it is a specific theme, or a certain style, or a clever arrangement of differently sized pieces, all of the work should flow together from one piece to the next.

Keep in mind, too, that different venues draw different crowds. If possible, find out the type of traffic that comes to a particular show and select pieces for display that you think will appeal to the people who will attend the show. This includes making sure that you don't display the $25,000 12-foot tall sculpture at a weekend street fair. The price point is wrong, and you'll probably overwhelm your booth space, and maybe even your booth neighbor's as well.

If you have other works but they don't fit your current exhibit theme or style, here's a solution: have a portfolio in your booth with photos of all of your other works. You can group them by styles, media, or in chronological order. That way people can flip through the book and see your other work without it being a distraction in your display.

An inexpensive way to create a portfolio is to use a three-ring binder with plastic protector pages to hold the photos. A more professional solution is to use an artist portfolio book. Either way you can add or remove photos as needed so that all your work is available for perusal, even if the piece itself didn't make the trip. Be sure to include information about each piece as well so that someone looking at your portfolio doesn't need to keep asking you "how much is it?" or "how big is it?"

Action Step

Look at photos of your display. Does it look cluttered? Are there paintings filling every square inch of space? If so, cull some of it. It's okay to put extra inventory in print bins.

If you don't have photos of your display...Why not?!?!? Start taking them at your next opportunity. Even a cell-phone photo is okay. Look at your display after the show in a more dispassionate frame of mind. Sometimes, what seems fine when you're newly set up and excited about a show can look different or awkward to you when you aren't right in front of it.

Mistake #5: Trying to please everyone by working in a theme or style that you know nothing about

One day I was sitting at my gallery when a lady walked in. She was an artist and wanted to be in my gallery. She asked if I would look at her portfolio. Since it wasn't a busy day, I did. Her work was nicely executed, very traditional acrylic paintings. None of the work really went with the fun and whimsical theme of my gallery. When I pointed this out to her she said, "Oh, I can paint whatever you want."

Now, based on the work in her portfolio, she certainly had a wide range of subject matter. And while she was skilled, most of her work lacked something. It lacked soul. The few pieces that had "personality" were the paintings of dogs. It turned out they were her dogs. She knew that subject matter very well and was able to portray it in an interesting and compelling way. The rest of her work was paintings of places she had never been or things she had never done. These pieces were just not that compelling and I did not accept her as one of my artists. Her portfolio made it look like she was trying to please everyone by showing any and all possible styles and themes. I am guessing that she ended up pleasing no one ... except herself.

Don't deny who you are as an artist. Trying to produce work with only the intention of selling it will result in "hotel art." You know, that bland, boring one-dimensional art that you see in many hotels. It all looks the same. Create the art that speaks to you. Not everyone will like it, but that's the point. Your art will find its way to those who will appreciate it and resonate to it.

Personally, my main theme is music. Much of my art has some representation of musical instruments or musical symbols in it. I used to play the violin. I took music lessons when I was young. I know enough about music so I don't put the treble clef backwards. With music as my theme, I am drawn to other artists who also do music-themed art. I have actually seen music themed art where the musical instruments or the musical symbols were either backwards or upside down and it wasn't purposely part of the design. The artist just didn't know enough about music to know that it was wrong.

If you are going to portray a theme, a place, or an object in your work, learn about it. Go to the place. Learn about the object. Study the theme.

Action Step
Research your subject matter before you begin a piece. Even if you are familiar with the theme, a refresher will help you fix it in your mind so your "creative self" can really grab onto it.

Mistake #6: Perfectionism

Think back to the first time you rode a bike. Were you able to ride it on your very first try?

Probably not. It took some practice. Maybe even some training wheels. But you kept at it. You kept falling. And you kept getting back on that bike because you were determined to ride it. Maybe you even had some help along the way. Eventually you were able to ride all by yourself without the training wheels. And didn't that feel great!

Your art is the same way. It's not going to be perfect the first time, or even the second time, or even the third time.

It takes practice to get it the way you want it. (Notice I did not say "It takes practice to get it right." Whatever your vision for that piece is the "right" way to create it.)

One of the problems many artists have is that they aren't able to immediately get the vision they have in their head onto the canvas, or clay, or fiber, or whatever the medium.

Maybe the necessary skills have not yet been developed. Or maybe the vision isn't clear enough. Or maybe the wrong materials are being used. Whatever the reason, the vision of the piece you have in your head is not what is coming out.

When this happens you may start making excuses. You may procrastinate. You may get to the point where you are so afraid of making a mistake that you don't create anything at all.

Don't fall into this trap.

Part of the creative process is to make mistakes. Even this book required several drafts, and the help of outside perspectives before it was complete. This is how you learn. The more mistakes you make the closer you come to creating that masterpiece.

Action Step
Keep practicing! Maybe the first try didn't turn out the way you imagined it. Try it again. And again. And again.

Mistake #7: Making assumptions

The dictionary definition of the verb "to assume" is, "to accept that something is true without checking or confirming it." As humans, we make all kinds of assumptions. As artists, we have even more to choose from.

Rejection is a big part of the life of an artist. It can be debilitating. It can cause you to make the assumption that your work is not good enough. Let's go back to the definition. Is it true that your work is not good enough? How do you know? Who says so?

When you were a kid, what happened to the art that you brought home from school? Most likely, it went up on the refrigerator. There was never any question of it being good enough.

Now, fast forward. As you have grown up, you have had lots of limitations, restrictions, and boundaries placed around you. You have taken all of that in and made it a part of you. Those limitations, restrictions, and boundaries have made you feel vulnerable. Feeling vulnerable, you become more susceptible to making assumptions, and usually negative ones. Assumptions like: "My work isn't good enough." Or, "I won't get through the jury process." Or, "I'll never sell that piece at that high of a price." Or, "They won't give me the booth space I want." Or, "My work isn't perfect."

Are these negative assumptions really true?

Another definition of "to assume" is, "to adopt or take on a quality." As in, to assume a mantle of success.

So, what if you change those assumptions from negative into positive? Instead of saying, "My work isn't good enough," what if you turn it around and ask, "If my work isn't good enough, what can I do to make it better?" Or, "Who says my work isn't good enough?" Or, "What is it about my work that makes me feel that it isn't good enough and what can I do about it?" Or, "What does 'not good enough' really mean?" Or even, "My work really is good, but it just wasn't right for that particular event."

It is time to shatter those assumptions. Question them. Ask if they are really true. Determine what it is that is causing you to make those assumptions in the first place and deal with those assumptions one by one until you discover that either your work is "good enough" or you need to improve it. Just be sure to be honest with yourself. It's good to have dreams and goals, but sometimes the hardest thing to confront is having an assumption that is unrealistically optimistic. The operative word here is "unrealistically". Only you can decide what is realistic. For example, it is unlikely that someone who just started painting last month is going to get a work accepted into The Louvre. Could it happen? Sure. Keep in mind that every person who ever had a big dream has been told "Oh, that's unrealistic." If you really believe in yourself, you can make the necessary effort to become what you dream.

Action Step
Every time one of those negative assumptions comes up in your mind, question it.

Mistake #8: Taking things personally

The art that you create is a very personal thing. It came from your heart and soul. You are proud of these things you have labored to bring into being. You love your creations. And you think that everyone else should love your creations too.

Wrong!

Have you ever heard someone at a show say something like, "That's nice, but I like Kincade better." Or how about, "My kid can paint better than that." Or maybe, "How much for just the frame?"

Ouch!

At first glance, these all sound like insults. It sounds like the person doesn't like your art. These comments even sound rude. Do not take them as such! Understand that not everyone has the same tastes. And not everyone is educated about art. People will say comments about your work like this because they are giving their honest reaction.

Consider this: at least you got a reaction. Getting a comment about your work whether it is positive or negative is good. You caused people to stop and look at your work. You may have even given them reason to think about your work. Whatever their reaction, treat it as a way to have a conversation with them. Find out why they like it or dislike it. Most importantly, don't take comments like this personally.

Another place where artists tend to take things personally is during the jury process. If you have ever received that skinny envelope with the one page letter that starts out, "Thank you for your submission," you may have experienced that sinking feeling or that dejection. Your brain goes through all kinds of thoughts like "My work isn't good enough," "They didn't pick me because I annoyed one of the jurors," "Why did HE get in and I didn't?" "They don't want me in that show because I'm not a famous artist." And on and on like this.

Let me repeat, do not take it personally.

A jury accepts work based on a number of criteria. It may be that the show already has too many artists in your medium. It could be that your art didn't fit what they were looking for. It could be that you sent your application in too late. There are many reasons why art is not accepted into a show or exhibit. It is not that there is anything "wrong" with your art.

Action Step
Time to work on your self-esteem. Start by showing your work to people you know and trust. Get feedback from those who will support you in your artistic endeavors. Just remember, not everyone is going to like your work. Keep in mind that the detractors are not your audience. There are plenty of positive supportive people out in the world who are part of your audience. Think of them when you need a boost.

Mistake #9: Not having a plan

Not having a plan is like getting in the car and not knowing where you are going. It might be fun to ride around for a while, but eventually you will need to find a place to eat, to get gas, or to sleep.

Not having a plan for your art career is similar. For a while it can be fun just to play around with lots of different styles or media. Experimenting can lead to interesting discoveries. Eventually, however, you will end up with a house full of art that you need to do something with.

So, before you go off on too many tangents, ask yourself a few questions:

- What do I want to do with my art?
- Why do I create art?
- Do I want to sell it at art shows?
- Do I want to get my work into a gallery?
- Do I want to have someone else sell my work for me?
- Do I want to sell my work online?
- Do I want to get my work into museums?
- What style or theme am I most passionate about?
- What techniques am I the best at?
- What medium is my favorite?
- What do I most enjoy creating?
- What techniques do I need to learn to improve my art?
- Do I want to teach classes?
- How much competition do I have?
- What can I do to give my work an edge over the competition?
- How will I market and publicize my work?

- What do I need to do in order to get my work into the marketplace?
- How am I going to identify and find my collectors?
- How will I cultivate my collectors?

There are no right or wrong answers to these questions. They are all questions to get you thinking about what you want to do with your art. Use the answers to these questions, along with any other information applicable to your art, to come up with a plan on how you want to grow your art career.

Remember, this plan is not written in stone. It can change as your grow and mature into your art career. Revisit it periodically and make changes as necessary.

Use this plan as a way to keep you focused. Whenever you see that "bright shiny object" ask yourself if it fits with the plan. If not, either discard it or save it for some later time.

Action Step
Answer any or all of the above questions. Put the answers in writing. Give yourself a clear picture of what you are working toward in your art career. If you want to write a formal business plan, use the educational resources available at the U. S. Small Business Administration website at https://www.sba.gov/

Mistake #10: Not documenting your work

Finishing a piece is always an exciting time. The piece is done and you are ready to show it to the world. If you haven't already come up with a title for this new masterpiece, now is the time to do so. Now that you have a finished titled piece, that is the end of the process, right?

Wrong! Now is the time to document your work. You need to keep a record of the works you have created. There are several reasons for this. First, so you can later look back fondly at your body of work. Second, so that you know when a piece was completed. Third, so that you know where a piece went. Fourth, so that you have all the information you need to file a copyright. Fifth, so that you have all the information readily available for exhibit submission.

Think of this almost like a ship's log. Fill it with lots of details about people, places, and things. Here are some suggestions:

- Title
- Date started
- Date completed
- Date sold
- Sold to whom?
- Price
- Places exhibited
- Inspiration
- Subject matter details (name, location, object)
- Techniques used
- Style
- Medium
- original digital image file name and location

Modify this list to suit your type of work. Include a photograph or two. You can even keep all of this information in the comment section of the digital image file properties.

So, what happens if you never kept any of this information for any of the work you have created? Do the best you can. Photographs are the best place to start and the most important piece. The visual image of the work may jog your memory. If you keep a receipt book from selling at shows, you may be able to glean some of the information from there.

Action Step
Create a log of your art.

Start with your current inventory. Once you have the information for your current works, go back to your older pieces and try to remember as much as you can about them.

Bonus Mistake: Bright Shiny Object Syndrome

Do you suffer from BSOS, otherwise known as Bright Shiny Object Syndrome?

Many creative types suffer from this malady. It manifests itself in an attraction to some new thing, whether it's a new tool, a new technique, or a new medium.

As an artist, you might see some new technique demonstrated and you want to try it. You are attracted to the newness, to the idea that this might be something you might enjoy doing. While that may be true, there is a price to be paid. You will have to spend time learning that new technique in order to become proficient at it. You will have to give up time practicing on your current technique.

Is it worth it?

Or you may see some new tool that looks really interesting. Again, you will have to spend time learning to use this new tool. Is this new tool really going to contribute to the quality of your work?

And what about a new medium? This could be a potentially radical shift. To make this drastic of a switch could potentially require an extensive amount of time and effort to learn and master.

While it is good to learn new things and to find new tools and techniques to improve your work, you must use caution. You do not want to keep jumping around from new idea to new idea without ever mastering any. You could end up becoming a perpetual student rather than a professional artist.

If you find yourself falling into this trap, ask yourself these questions:

- Will this help improve my current body of work?
- Can I be disciplined enough to keep at this new thing until I am sufficiently expert at it without jeopardizing my other work?

Action Step
Focus on one technique or style that you are passionate about and master it before moving on to the next.

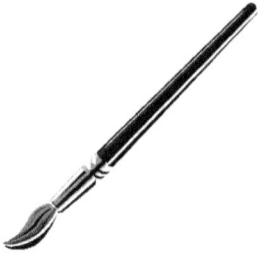

Next Steps

So, are you guilty of committing any of these mistakes? I will now admit it…I have done every single one of these. If you see yourself in any of these, follow the action step at the end of that chapter to correct your mistake.

It is my sincere hope that once you make any needed corrections, your art and your art sales will improve.

For more artist and crafter resources visit
http://www.TheShyArtist.com

Bonus – Newsletter Topic Ideas

Visit: **www.theshyartist.com/mistakes**

and download your free list of newsletter/blog/social media topic ideas.

About the author:

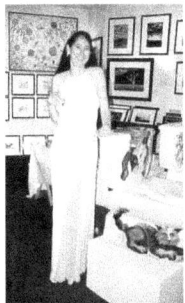

Loretta Alvarado is the owner of How Original! Art Gallery. She has been doing arts & crafts shows for over 20 years. She now owns TheShyArtist.com, an online resource of instructional guides and videos for artists who need help overcoming shyness so they can make more sales.

Connect with me:

Website: http://www.theshyartist.com/

Facebook: http://www.facebook.com/TheShyArtist

Blog: http://www.theshyartist.com/blog.html

Pinterest: http://pinterest.com/theshyartist/